Things That STING

Scorpions

By Therese Shea

 Gareth Stevens
PUBLISHING

Please visit our website, www.garethstevens.com. For a free color catalog of all our high-quality books, call toll free 1-000-542-2595 or fax 1-877-542-2596.

Library of Congress Cataloging-in-Publication Data

Shea, Therese.
Scorpions / by Therese Shea.
p. cm. — (Things that sting)
Includes index.
ISBN 978-1-4824-1715-9 (pbk.)
ISBN 978-1-4824-1716-6 (6-pack)
ISBN 978-1-4824-1714-2 (library binding)
1. Scorpions — Juvenile literature. I. Shea, Therese. II. Title.
QL458.4 S54 2015

First Edition

Published in 2016 by
Gareth Stevens Publishing
111 East 14th Street, Suite 349
New York, NY 10003

Copyright © 2016 Gareth Stevens Publishing

Designer: Michael J. Flynn
Editor: Therese Shea

Photo credits: Cover, p. 1 wacpan/Shutterstock.com; p. 5 Wanchai Orsuk/Shutterstock.com; p. 7 ekler/Shutterstock.com; p. 9 (scorpion) Marek R. Swadzba/Shutterstock.com; p. 9 (tick, spider) Henrik Larsson/Shutterstock.com; p. 9 (daddy longlegs) Butterfly Hunter/Shutterstock.com; p. 9 (mite) D. Kucharski K. Kucharska/Shutterstock.com; p. 11 Wayne Lynch/All Canada Photos/Getty Images; p. 13 Andy Park/Oxford Scientific/Getty Images; p. 15 Milan Vachal/Shutterstock.com; p. 17 reptiles4all/Shutterstock.com; p. 19 Abraham Badenhorst/Shutterstock.com; p. 21 EcoPrint/Shutterstock.com.

Printed in the United States of America

CPSIA compliance information: Batch #CS15GS: For further information contact Gareth Stevens, New York, New York at 1-800-542-2595.

Contents

Words in the glossary appear in **bold** type the first time they are used in the text.

Built to Kill

Scorpions are built to kill—and they look like it. A scorpion has large **pincers** to seize and smash prey, and a long, curving tail that ends with a stinger. These features and the scorpion's deadly poison, called venom, make it a fearsome predator.

You might be surprised to learn that scorpions aren't a single kind of animal. In fact, there are about 1,500 kinds, or species, of scorpions. All are venomous. Are you brave enough to read more about these scary stingers?

That Smarts!

Scorpions are ancient! The first ones were around more than 400 million years ago.

Luckily for us, scorpions mostly like to eat insects!

They're Everywhere!

Most kinds of scorpions live in deserts, but many also live in places such as grasslands, forests, and mountains. Scorpion coloring tends to match their surroundings. For example, scorpions in sandy deserts are light colored.

Different species of scorpions are different sizes. The longest scorpion, the rock scorpion of South Africa, can grow to be more than 8 inches (20 cm) long. However, one species found in the Caribbean only grows to be about 0.5 inch (1.3 cm) long.

That smarts!

One **fossil** of an ancient scorpion was about 3.3 feet (1 M) long. The pincer fossil of a sea scorpion that could have been about 8.2 feet (2.5 M) long has also been found!

Scorpions: Where They Live

Scorpions live on every big landmass on Earth except Greenland and Antarctica.

GREENLAND

NORTH
AMERICA

EUROPE

ASIA

AFRICA

SOUTH
AMERICA

AUSTRALIA

- where scorpions live

ANTARCTICA

Terrifying Tail

Scorpions are a kind of arachnid (uh-RAK-nihd). Spiders, daddy longlegs, mites, and ticks are all arachnids, too. Like other arachnids, scorpions have eight legs and a tough exoskeleton, which is the name for their hard outer covering.

Unlike most other arachnids, scorpions have a long, **flexible** tail attached to the rear part of their body. The tail contains body parts called glands that produce venom and ends in a sharp stinger. The tail and stinger are used to attack prey as well as to fight off predators.

That Smarts!

The exoskeleton of scorpions is made up of matter called chitin [KY-tuhn]. It's similar to what makes up our fingernails.

Arachnids are **arthropods**. Most arachnids, such as scorpions, eat smaller arthropods.

mite

spider

tick

daddy longlegs

A Serious Sting

Scorpions have a large pair of pincers, called pedipalps, to hold on to their prey. However, the pedipalps aren't that strong, so venom is necessary to stop prey from getting away. When a scorpion stings an animal, venom flows out of the stinger and into the animal. The venom either kills the animal or **paralyzes** it. This gives the scorpion time to eat.

Scientists have discovered that scorpion species with larger pedipalps have weaker venom and species with smaller pedipalps have stronger venom.

THAT SMARTS!

Male scorpions have longer tails than female scorpions.

Scorpions don't have to worry about holding on to prey for too long because of their powerful venom. Pedipalps are also used to crush smaller prey such as insects.

Liquid Lunch

What happens once scorpions have their prey? Scorpions don't have jaws like people do. They "drink" their food. They use a pair of toothed body parts called chelicerae (kih-LIH-suh-ree) to cut into prey.

Next, liquids from within the scorpion's body are **secreted** into the prey. This matter turns the inside of the prey's body into a liquid. It's easy for the scorpion to suck the liquid into its own body. All this can take several hours!

That Smarts!

Most scorpion venom is just enough to cause a painful bump on a person's skin. However, about 25 species of scorpions have venom powerful enough to kill a person.

This scorpion is slowly eating a cockroach.

13

Midnight Snack

Scorpions are nocturnal. That means they're mostly active at night. They avoid heat and sunlight by spending most of their time in a **burrow**. They come out when they're hungry. Besides insects, scorpions may eat lizards, snakes, and **rodents**.

Scorpions can't see very well. They have tiny hairs on their legs that can feel **vibrations**. A scorpion often waits underground until it feels vibrations of prey above. Then it quickly pops out of the burrow and strikes. Scorpions can even feel vibrations in the air if an insect is flying nearby.

THAT SMARTS!

At least one species of scorpion doesn't even leave its burrow. It waits for prey to come to it!

Scorpions are carnivores. That means they eat meat.

Scorplings

Scorpions spend most of their lives alone. However, male scorpions leave their burrows to look for a female to **mate** with. After mating, the male usually leaves. If he doesn't, the female may kill and eat him!

The female scorpion then has between 1 and 100 live babies. Baby scorpions, called scorplings, ride on their mother's back for up to 50 days. As they grow, they **molt** their exoskeleton. After a scorpling's first molt, it leaves its mother's back and finds new territory to hunt.

THAT SMARTS!

There are at least two types of scorpions able to produce babies without a mate.

Scorpions may molt up to nine times before they're fully grown.

Enemies

As deadly as scorpions can be, they do have predators. In fact, their venom doesn't affect some predators. These predators may even break off a scorpion's tail! Birds, lizards, snakes, rodents, bats, and frogs hunt scorpions. Large spiders and centipedes also eat them.

Scorpions may eat each other, even if they're the same species. It's thought they do this so they'll have larger territories in which to hunt. In fact, mother scorpions may eat their own babies!

THAT smarts!

In some parts of the world, people eat scorpions!

Birds can watch for scorpions from above and grab them as they leave their burrow.

Survivalists

Scorpions can avoid their predators by not leaving their burrow very much. In fact, some species can live on just one insect a year. They're not spotted eating in the wild very often.

Scorpions are experts at staying alive in hard conditions. Those that live in places that get cold **hibernate** through winter. When prey comes by, though, they snap back into action.

In a study, scientists froze several scorpions. After warming up in the sun, the scorpions came back to life! These arachnids are truly amazing—just don't get too close!

That Smarts!

Most species of scorpions live between 4 and 25 years.

WHY SO DEADLY?

stinger wounds skin and delivers venom

venom glands make venom to paralyze or kill prey

pedipalps seize and smash prey

chelicerae cut prey

Glossary

arthropod: an animal that lacks a backbone and has a skeleton on the outside of its body, such as an insect, spider, shrimp, or crab

burrow: a hole made by an animal in which it lives or hides

flexible: able to bend easily

fossil: the hardened marks or remains of plants and animals that formed over thousands or millions of years

hibernate: to be in a sleeplike state for an extended period of time, usually during winter

mate: to come together to make babies

molt: to shed an exoskeleton

paralyze: to make something lose the ability to move

pincer: a front claw on some animals that is used to hold things

rodent: a small, furry animal with large front teeth, such as a mouse or rat

secrete: to produce and release

vibration: a rapid movement back and forth

For More Information

Books

Ganeri, Anita. *Scorpion*. Chicago, IL: Heinemann Library, 2011.

Owings, Lisa. *The Deathstalker Scorpion*. Minneapolis, MN: Bellwether Media, Inc., 2013.

Thomas, Isabel. *Scorpion vs. Tarantula*. Chicago, IL: Raintree, 2006.

Websites

Arachnids
www.bbc.co.uk/nature/life/Arachnid
Learn more about scorpions and other arachnids from this website's fascinating vidoes.

Scorpion Pictures
www.scorpionworlds.com/scorpion-pictures/
See photos of many species of scorpions, and find links to more information.

Index